Visit Nick Arnold at
www.nickarnold-website.com

Scholastic Children's Books,
Euston House, 24 Eversholt Street,
London, NW1 1DB, UK

A division of Scholastic Ltd
London ~ New York ~ Toronto ~ Sydney ~ Auckland
Mexico City ~ New Delhi ~ Hong Kong

First published in the UK by Scholastic Ltd, 2007

Text copyright © Nick Arnold, 2007
Cover illustration © Tony De Saulles, 2007
Inside illustrations by Dave Smith, based on the style of the original
Horrible Science artwork by Tony De Saulles
Illustrations © Dave Smith 2007
All rights reserved

10 digit ISBN 0 439 94407 4
13 digit ISBN 978 0439 94407 6

Printed and bound by Tien Wah Press Pte. Ltd, Malaysia

2 4 6 8 10 9 7 5 3 1

CONTENTS

READ ON –
IT GETS WORSE!

INTRODUCTION

Science is full of mysteries, but the biggest mystery of all is where it all comes from. I mean, who thought up all those science facts that you're forced to learn in school? Was it your teachers?

NOT ME...

OR ME!

No – the people you have to blame are famous scientists through the ages. They used experiments to find out the facts that you have to learn. Now any old science book will tell you all about these great geniuses – but this book goes further. It's a Horrible Handbook – so it shows you how to follow in the great scientists' footsteps, with activities based on their famous experiments.

Why not try a few? You might not become a science superstar, but I guarantee you'll be a famously foul expert!

A SICKENING
START

Talking about things horrible, this is famous mad scientist Baron Frankenstein and the monster boy he made from bits of human body...

I'M THRILLED TO BITS TO MEET YOU!

AND I'M MADE FROM BITS.

The Baron lists his hobbies as performing evil experiments and testing revolting home remedies on Monster Boy. And Monster Boy says he enjoys digging up bodies, making up terrible jokes and scaring the cat. Anyway, the Baron and Monster Boy are here to guide us through the experiments and tell us about the famous scientists. If Monster Boy can stay awake – that is!

WAKE UP, MONSTER BOY!

YOU HAVEN'T READ THE SAFETY RULES!

BARON FRANKENSTEIN'S FAMOUSLY FOUL EXPERIMENT SAFETY RULES

1 Always read an experiment before you try it. Make sure you have every item of equipment. Here are some items you'll be using quite a lot...

BLU TACK, MEASURING JUG, TAPE MEASURE, STICKY TAPE, BALLOONS, RULER, PET ADULT, NOTEBOOK AND PENCIL

And here are some more items that I, Baron Frankenstein, consider vital:

SHOVEL FOR DIGGING UP BODIES, THUMBSCREWS TO TORTURE VICTIMS, SELECTION OF SAWS FOR CUTTING OFF BODY BITS, BOTTLE OF BLOOD IN CASE MONSTER BOY GETS THIRSTY!

2 Always read the warning signs...

HORRIBLE DANGER WARNING!

Clear little brothers and sisters out of harm's way (if they won't move tell them that you'll set Monster Boy on them). Younger readers should order their pet adult to do the more dangerous jobs.

HORRIBLE MESS WARNING!

Try not to leave blood (or any other messy bits) all over your laboratory.

3 Always clear up after your experiments.

This will keep your pet adult happy (they do have feelings, you know).

READY TO START?

The Awful Ancients

In ancient times people knew nothing about science, in fact they were even more ignorant than you were on your first day at school. But that's when certain brainy boffins took the first faltering steps to invent science and (oh yikes!) maths…

THE WOBBLY EARTH

I AM GOING TO SHOW YOU AN EXPERIMENT BASED ON THE IDEAS OF THALES. HE THOUGHT THE EARTH FLOATED ON WATER.

HE MUST HAVE BEEN A BIT WET.

BRAINY BREAKTHROUGH

Name: THALES OF MILETUS (625-547 BC)
Nationality: GREEK (BORN IN MODERN TURKEY)

Before Thales, people thought everything was caused by gods. But Thales wanted to find natural explanations based on observation and reason. He didn't do experiments but many people reckon he was the world's first scientist. Here's how talented Thales imagined the world...

WHAT YOU NEED:

- **Glass bowl 15–20 cm across**
- **Clingfilm**
- **Empty film canister or similar light object**
- **Large wooden spoon**

ACTUALLY I PREFER A VAT OF BLOOD, SOME SKIN AND A FEW BONES.

WHAT YOU DO:

1 Fill the bowl with water almost to the top.

NOW FOR THE FUN BIT!

2 Float a piece of clingfilm on top of the water. The clingfilm should almost touch the sides of the bowl but not quite.

3 Take the lid off the film canister and place it upside down on the clingfilm. Great – you've now built a tower on the water-world Thales imagined.

4 Make an earthquake by tapping the side of the bowl with the side of the wooden spoon.

WHAT HAPPENS:

The tower sways. If you hit the bowl hard enough the tower will fall.

THIS IS BECAUSE:

Your tapping sets off waves of motion through the water that hit the clingfilm and make the tower sway. Scientists know that the landmasses float on melted rock deep underground. Currents in the rock jostle the landmasses causing earthquakes. So in a way, the Earth is floating and Thales' water idea wasn't so wet after all.

AN EARTH-SHAKING DISCOVERY

HENG ZHANG MEASURED THE SHAKING OF AN EARTHQUAKE.

HE HAD A SHAKY GRASP OF SCIENCE...

BRAINY BREAKTHROUGH

NAME: HENG ZHANG
(AD78-139)
NATIONALITY: CHINESE

Most experiments need equipment to detect, time or measure the effect you're trying to study. Heng Zhang is famous for building one of the first items of scientific equipment – a seismograph for detecting earthquake shockwaves. Fancy making your own?

WHAT YOU NEED:
- Doorway
- 2 metres of string
- Drawing pin
- Felt pen
- Two 30-cm rulers
- Crocodile or alligator clip

HOW ABOUT A REAL ALLIGATOR?

BAD IDEA!

• 3-4 pieces of paper stuck together lengthways like this

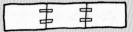

• Or a long length of greaseproof paper
• Blu tack or modelling clay

• Large rectangular plastic storage box
• A good friend or pet adult

I'M A BIT STUCK UP!

WHAT YOU DO:

1 Set up the experiment (younger readers will probably need the help of their pet adult)…

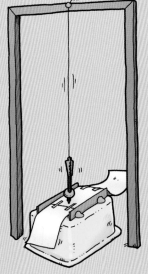

2 Use blu tack to stick two corners on one side of your box to the floor. (If you have carpets you may need to lay down a large sheet of cardboard and stick the box to this.)

3 Use more blu tack to stick the two rulers on their sides on top of the box as shown. They should be just far enough apart for your paper to rest between them.

4 Now for the exciting bit. Ask your pet adult to slowly pull the paper towards them. The pen should draw a fairly straight line on the paper.

5 Repeat step 4, but this time you should slap the side of the box where the corners aren't stuck down.

WHAT HAPPENS:
Your line becomes jerky – it might even zigzag.

THIS IS BECAUSE:
Ever tried to write in a moving car? You might hold your pen ever-so steady but because the vehicle is moving, your writing is all over the place. A modern seismograph works in the same way. The pen is steady, but as the ground moves so does the paper and a zigzag line is produced. Heng Zhang's seismograph was a bit more basic and here it is...

When a quake occurred, the shockwaves dislodged a ball from a dragon's mouth and it fell into a frog's mouth. In fact Heng's machine detected an earthquake and pinpointed its direction over 1,000 km away. Clever huh?

Bet you never knew!
Heng Zhang could have been a top government minister but he turned down promotion to work on science. So what would you give up for science homework? On second thoughts – maybe I shouldn't ask!

I DON'T BE-LEVER IT!

Monster boy is showing the cat the principle of the lever as discovered by Archimedes…

WHAT YOU NEED:

- Wooden ruler or piece of wood 30 cm long
- Heavy book (we're talking boring books here NOT Horrible Science books!)
- Table • Kitchen scales
- Notebook and pencil
- Toy bucket (the sort of thing your little brother or sister plays with on the beach) • Measuring jug – for this experiment you can assume 100 ml of water weighs 100 grams

WHAT YOU DO:

1 Weigh the book on your scales and note the result.

2 The ruler is going to be your lever. Set up the experiment like this...

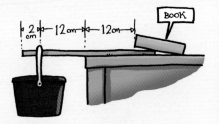

3 Slowly add water to the bucket until the book starts to tip up. Weigh the bucket and the water it contains and note down your figure.

4 Tip away the water and set up the experiment like this...

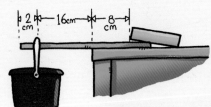

5 Repeat Step 3.

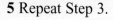

WHAT HAPPENS:

The first time you weighed the bucket of water it weighed as much as the book. The second time, the bucket of water weighed half as much.

THIS IS BECAUSE:

Here's the experiment again with a few vital science words added:

Archimedes' law says:

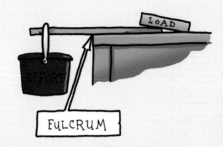

> Effort weight x distance from the fulcrum = load weight x distance from the fulcrum

That means if you double the distance of the effort from the fulcrum, you can halve the weight of the effort you need to lift the load. And that's why in steps 4 and 5 you only needed half the weight in the bucket. Archimedes' law helped people develop a vast range of inventions that use levers — everything from cranes to nutcrackers…

OR EVEN MY HOMEMADE BONE-CRACKER!

Bet you never knew!

1 Archimedes probably didn't experiment with levers, but later when his home city was under attack by the Romans, he devised a giant lever called "the claw". The lethal lever lifted ships in the air so that their crews fell and got dashed to bits on the rocks.

2 Archimedes discovered 13 new solid shapes. Some of them had weird names — I bet your teacher's never heard of the 30-sided rhombicosidododecahedron (rom-bicko-si-do-doe-deck-a-he-dron) — but you just have!

A WEIGHTY MATTER

OUR NEXT EXPERIMENT IS ABOUT FLOATING...

IS THAT WHY THERE'S AN EYEBALL FLOATING IN MY SOUP?

BRAINY BREAKTHROUGH

NAME: ARCHIMEDES
(yes, him again)

Archimedes didn't just make sense of levers – he invented a new kind of pulley, a water-raising screw, and discovered the law of buoyancy – the reason why things float. Why not climb aboard the next experiment?

WHAT YOU NEED:

- Kitchen scales complete with a weighing pan
- Screw-top jar (I used a plastic paperclip jar)
- Glass or glass jar large enough to hold the screw-top jar
- Some weights – I used small batteries
- Measuring jug
- Notebook and pencil

AND I USED AN EYEBALL JAR!

HORRIBLE MESS!
Water may get spilt. Mop up any spills – otherwise you'll face a few unwelcome thrills and spills from your parents.

WHAT YOU DO:

1 Put some weights in your jar, replace the lid and place it in a sink of water. Ideally the jar should just float with its lid level with the water. You might need to adjust the weight to get this result.

2 Weigh your jar with the weights in and make a note of this figure.

3 Place a glass in the pan of the scales. Fill the glass up to the brim with water and note its weight.

4 Place your weighted jar in the water. Some of the water will overflow into the weighing pan. Make a note of the weight.

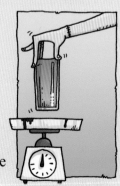

5 Remove the glass of water and jar. Make a note of the weight of water in the pan.

WHAT HAPPENS:

The weight of water that overflowed from the glass is equal to the weight of the screw-top jar.

THIS IS BECAUSE:

Archimedes said that when you put an object in water (and it could be anything from a supertanker to your big toe)...

OR SOMEONE ELSE'S BIG TOE!

... it will push aside its own volume (the space it takes up) of water. If the object weighs less than its volume of water it will float – and if it weighs more it will sink.

Bet you never knew!

Archimedes was doing sums when the Romans captured his city. He told a Roman soldier he was too busy to be bothered so the solider killed him instead. And after that the scientist was too dead to be bothered about anything.

ERK...

Feeling the Force

A force is the power to make an object move in a certain direction. So when you get shoved into school or shoved into bed – well, that's a force…

Anyway all the experiments in this chapter are to do with objects moving under the influence of forces and all you have to do is force yourself to try them!

OOF!

WHO'S THE FALL GUY?

WHAT GOES UP MUST COME DOWN – BUT HOW FAST? BEFORE GALILEO PEOPLE THOUGHT HEAVIER OBJECTS FELL FASTER.

I BET THEY WERE FALLING DOWN ON THE JOB.

BRAINY BREAKTHROUGH

NAME: GALILEO GALILEI (1564–1642)
NATIONALITY: ITALIAN

Science superstar Galileo used experiments to explain how a pendulum swings and how cannonballs whizz through the air. And he used a telescope to back claims by Polish astronomer Nicolaus Copernicus (1473–1543) that the Earth moves round the Sun. But the Church disagreed and gallant Galileo was locked up for the rest of his life. Here's Galileo's most famous experiment – measuring the force of gravity. Try it and you'll be on a roll!

WHAT YOU NEED:

- Parcel tape and scissors
- Bucket about 24 cm high
- Larger bucket
- Metal ballbearing
- Notebook and pencil
- Plank of wood 2.5 metres long and at least 12 cm wide
- Marble or rubber ball of the same size as the ballbearing
- Two strips of wood – ideally as long as the plank
- Stopwatch or watch with a second hand
- Good friend or pet adult

WHAT YOU DO:

1 Turn the smaller bucket upside-down and rest one end of the plank on it.

2 Using the parcel tape, stick the strips of wood to make a narrow lane running down the plank. The gap between the two strips of wood should be wide enough to allow the balls to easily roll down the plank between them. This is going to be your ball-run.

YOU COULD USE A LENGTH OF PLASTIC GUTTERING INSTEAD OF THE PLANK AND WOOD STRIPS...

3 Place the bucket on its side at the end of the plank to catch the balls when you roll them down.

4 Order your pet adult to time first the marble and then the ballbearing as you roll them down the ball-run.

5 Note their times. You may want to try a few more tests.

WHAT HAPPENS:

Both balls take the same time to reach the end of the plank. The heavier ball isn't faster.

THIS IS BECAUSE:

Before Galileo, people thought heavy objects fell faster than light objects. But by timing the speed of balls rolling down a slope, Galileo found that objects of the same size and shape fall at the same speed under the influence of gravity. Heavy objects don't fall faster.

Galileo was a genius because for the first time he combined all the features of modern experiments – equipment, observation, repeating the experiment to test the result and a mathematical explanation. What a star!

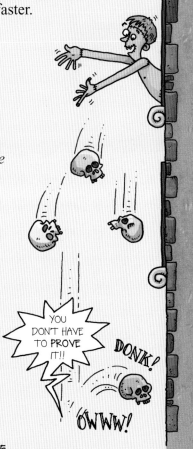

YOU DON'T HAVE TO PROVE IT!!

DONK!

OWWW!

A MOVING MOMENT

GALILEO MEASURED HOW OBJECTS FALL, BUT ISAAC NEWTON EXPLAINED THE WHOLE OF GRAVITY AND HE ALSO EXPLAINED HOW THINGS MOVED. SO GET MOVING WITH THIS EXPERIMENT!

SHOVE

GRUMBLE, WHINGE

BRAINY BREAKTHROUGH

NAME: ISAAC NEWTON (1642-1727)
NATIONALITY: BRITISH

Isaac Newton's book 'The Mathematical Principles of Natural Philosophy' sounds boring and a lot of people thought it was boring, especially as it was full of maths and written in Latin. But 99.9 per cent of scientists think it's the greatest book ever written. In it Newton explained gravity and how everything in the universe moves. He made his points with maths but experiments have proved him right, right and right again. I expect you're just about to prove him right too...

WHAT YOU NEED:

• Clean plastic tube 30–45 cm long, with an opening
1.2–2 cm across. If you haven't got a tube you could use
a piece of A4 paper • Pen • Sticky tape and scissors
• A piece of stiff paper 12 x 16 cm

WHAT YOU DO:

1 Roll the piece of stiff paper lengthways around the pen
and secure it with sticky tape to make a tube shape. This
is going to be your dart.

2 Make a nose cone for your dart by wrapping sticky
tape around one end of the dart to block it up.

3 The plastic tube is going to be your launch tube.
Alternatively, simply roll the A4 paper lengthwise
around your dart. You'll need to make your launch tube
a little wider than the dart. Secure the launch tube with
sticky tape.

4 Place the dart in the tube, take a deep breath and…

DON'T FIRE IT AT THE CAT!

WHAT HAPPENS:

When you blow through the launch tube the dart whizzes out of the other end.

THIS IS BECAUSE:

Here's how Newton explained what happens.

1 Newton's First Law of Motion – an object that isn't affected by a force stays where it is. A force makes the object move in a straight line until another force affects it.

DART STAYS STILL WHEN NOT IN USE

DART FLIES OFF IN STRAIGHT LINE UNTIL FORCE OF GRAVITY PULLS IT DOWN

2 Newton's Second Law of Motion – forces can make an object change speed or direction.

DART SLOWED BY FORCE OF AIR RUBBING AGAINST IT

MONSTER'S BREATH MAKES DART ZOOM OFF

NO, MONSTER BOY, THE SLOWING FORCE OF THE AIR IS NO EXCUSE FOR NOT DOING THE WASHING UP.

Bet you never knew!

If you had fired your dart in space it would have flown off in a straight line for ever — or until it bopped an alien. Newton's Third Law of Motion says that if you apply a force to anything it will push back just as hard. This sounds weird — but you can prove it. Stand with the left side of your body — foot, leg, hip and shoulder touching a wall. Push against the wall (try not to push it over!) Now try to raise your RIGHT foot. You can't! This is because the wall is pushing back, and if you raise your right foot the wall will push you over!

LOOKS LIKE YOU'RE A BIT OF A PUSHOVER.

So are you a pushover? Why not find out with this queasy quiz?

BOFFINS' BODY BITS Quiz

Which of these scientists' body bits have been studied by other scientists?

1. Copernicus' skull

2. Galileo's finger

3. Newton's eyeball

Answers:

1. Yes – in 2005 scientists found Copernicus' skull and used it to work out what he looked like. He had a broken nose and a scar and looked rather like a painting made in his lifetime.

2. Yes – Galileo's finger is on display in a museum of Florence, Italy. You can see that the great man didn't bite his fingernails.

3. No – although Newton was very proud of not having to wear glasses even when he was an old man.

And talking about seeing things, the next chapter is definitely worth seeing...

Seeing the Light

This chapter takes a look at light and seeing – well, you can't see much without light, can you? Eight hundred years ago they were both a bit of a mystery. You could say that people were in the dark about light, and it took some bright scientists to shine a bit of light on the subject…

A SIGHT FOR SORE EYES

SMILE – LET'S SEE YOUR FANGS!

IBN AL-HAYTHAM DISCOVERED THE PRINCIPLE BEHIND THE CAMERA BEFORE IT HAD EVEN BEEN INVENTED. I GUESS IT JUST CLICKED FOR HIM, HA HA!

BRAINY BREAKTHROUGH

NAME: IBN AL-HAYTHAM (AD965-1038)
NATIONALITY: BORN IN MODERN IRAQ

Ibn al-Haytham was the first person to suggest you see something when light reflects from that object into your eye. Before then many people thought that the eyes produced a ray to see things by. Ibn al-Haytham used maths and experiments to show that light travels in straight lines and it bends (refracts, as scientists say) as it passes through water. Here's a device that he built to help with his research...

WHAT YOU NEED:

- Sticky tape and scissors
- 4 sheets of black A4 paper – ideally non-shiny
- Container about 20–23 cm long – one of those crisps tubes is ideal
- 2 large elastic bands
- Drawing pin, small screwdriver, hammer and nail
- Greaseproof paper
- Pet adult
- Bright sunny day
- Room with thick, dark curtains

WAKE UP. IT'S TIME FOR THE EXPERIMENT!

WHAT YOU DO:

1 Use the drawing pin to make a hole in the middle of the bottom of the container. Use the hammer and nail and then the screwdriver to make the hole a little larger. The ideal size is 4–5 mm – don't make it bigger. Younger readers should order their pet adult to undertake this tricky task.

2 Take the lid off the container. Make a tube by rolling a sheet of black paper from top to bottom and place it inside the container. The tube should be as wide as the container.

3 Stretch a piece of greaseproof paper over the open end of the container and secure it with an elastic band.

4 Roll the other sheets of black paper into a tube and secure it with sticky tape. Then stick this black tube to the greaseproof paper end of the container.

5 So there it is – you've made a pinhole viewer – I hope the Sun is still shining! Peep the viewer out through the curtains and look through the black paper tube end.

WHAT HAPPENS:

You should see an upside-down, back-to-front view of the outside world.

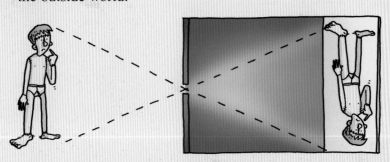

THIS IS BECAUSE:

You're looking at light that shone through the hole and is being projected on the greaseproof paper. As Ibn al-Haytham realized, light travels in straight lines, and that means light from the sky is projected on the bottom of the paper and light from the lower part of the scene makes it to the top of the paper, so you see the world upside down. Left and right are reversed in the same way. This is much the same way as a camera works, although there is film or a light sensor rather than paper at the back of the box.

Bet you never knew!

Ibn al-Haytham worked for a mad ruler of Egypt named al Hakim. The barking-mad monarch is said to have ordered that every dog in Egypt be killed because their barking upset him. In the end the scientist pretended to be mad in order to escape execution. Mind you, some scientists are genuinely mad…

TOOT

PARP

HA HA – I LOVE TO PLAY THE ORGAN MADLY AT MIDNIGHT!

YEP – HE'S A FRUITCAKE ALL RIGHT.

A COLOURFUL CHARACTER

ISAAC NEWTON DISCOVERED THAT SUNLIGHT CONTAINS ALL THE COLOURS OF THE RAINBOW...

HE PUT ALL THE OTHER SCIENTISTS IN THE SHADE!

BRAINY BREAKTHROUGH

NAME: ISAAC NEWTON (Yes, him again!)
NATIONALITY: BRITISH

Not content with discovering the laws of motion and gravity, Incredible Izzy also worked on light. I guess he made light work of it (groan!). Why not try the first part of Newton's famous light experiment – you might take a shine to it!

WHAT YOU NEED:

- A small mirror
- Bowl of water (the bowl must be deep enough to stand the mirror in it at an angle. A baking dish is ideal or you could try a shaving mirror and a washing-up bowl.
- Bright sunny day
- Room with very dark curtains
- Blu tack

I PREFER DARKNESS – IT'S MORE CREEPY!

WHAT YOU DO:

1 Close the curtains, allowing just a slit of sunlight into the room.

2 Place the bowl of water in the sunlight.

3 Place the mirror in the bowl at a shallow angle. If you're using a shaving mirror you can adjust the angle. If you use another mirror you can prop it against the side of the bowl and secure it with a blob of blu tack.

WHAT HAPPENS:

A rainbow appears on your wall or ceiling.

THIS IS BECAUSE:

Imagine sunlight is made of coloured threads. If you pick apart the threads you can see their separate colours. As the sunlight passed through the water, each colour of light was bent (refracted) at a different angle – pushing them apart. The mirror simply reflected the colours. Newton showed what was going on by measuring the angle at which each colour was refracted. Then he showed that each colour can't be refracted into more colours.

Bet you never knew!

We didn't try the second part of Newton's experiment because it's really hard to refract a pure colour from the rainbow – for one thing, the light's really dim.
No wonder scientist Robert Hooke didn't agree with Newton's findings. I bet they had some colourful words to say to each other...

SEEING IS BELIEVING

THOMAS YOUNG MUST HAVE BEEN THE BRAINIEST PERSON EVER...

WHAT – SMARTER THAN YOU?

GRRR! JUST GET ON WITH THE EXPERIMENT!

BRAINY BREAKTHROUGH

NAME: THOMAS YOUNG (1773-1829)
NATIONALITY: BRITISH

Thomas Young started reading when he was two. By the age of six he had read the Bible – twice. He went on to learn 12 languages and work out how to read ancient Egyptian (I expect that was his idea of light relief). But talking about light – today Young is most famous for proving that light is made up of waves and discovering how you see. And now you can too!

WHAT YOU NEED:

- **Waterproof felt-tip pens – black, red, and blue**
- **Small magnifying glass**
- **Sticky tape and scissors**
- **Clear polythene bag about 15 cm x 25 cm deep**

Tip for people who want everything in life to be easy – you can cheat by using a glass jar with a lid or even a goldfish bowl instead of the bag.

DON'T EAT THE GOLDFISH!

WHAT YOU DO:

1 Fill the bag with water and knot the neck so that the water can't escape. If you're using a jar or bowl you can simply fill it with water. Replace the lid, if it's a jar.

IRIS

PUPIL

2 This bag is your eyeball. You can draw on a few blood vessels and an iris. You need to draw the pupil as a black ring about 3 cm across. Don't colour in the pupil.

3 Put the back of the eyeball to your eye so you are looking through the eyeball and out of the pupil. Try looking out of the window.

4 Then use sticky tape to stick the magnifying glass over the pupil of your homemade eyeball.

5 Look out through the eyeball and out of the window again – you may need to move your head back a little.

WHAT HAPPENS:

Without the magnifying glass everything looks blurry. With the magnifying glass, especially if you move your head back, you'll see the scene clearly but it's upside down and back to front.

THIS IS BECAUSE:

Thomas Young did a number of experiments on his own eyeballs and found that the lens in your eyeball is necessary to see things in focus, even if the image that forms needs to be corrected by your brain.

LENS

Final proof came from testing a man who had lost his lens. Young found the man couldn't see clearly compared to a normal person. This kind of comparison is a key part of modern experiments...

Bet you never knew!

1 One of Young's experiments involved measuring his own eyeballs. To do this he stuck a special tool around his eyeball and took the measurement from the back of his eye socket – erk!

2 As a teenager Thomas Young believed he was dying of a fatal lung disease. But instead of despairing he wrote a scientific book describing the effects of his deadly disease.

Gasping Gases

Remember the last time you were breathless? Maybe it was when you tried to test your teacher and had to run for your life. When you're out of breath your body's demanding more oxygen from the air. But air has other horribly interesting secrets, as scientists found out...

COUGH

SPLUTTER

PUFF BANG

FUTT FUTT

UNDER PRESSURE

IN THIS EXPERIMENT I WILL TEACH YOU ABOUT NOTHING.

BUT I KNOW NOTHING ALREADY!

GRR— FOOLISH BOY!

BRAINY BREAKTHROUGH

NAME: OTTO VON GUERICKE (1602-1686)
NATIONALITY: GERMAN

Otto von Guericke was very interested in nothing. Or to be more exact, he was interested in pumping air out of containers so that there was nothing inside them. Why not try a similar experiment — you'll find there's nothing to it!

SUCK

WHAT YOU NEED:

• 2-litre plastic drink bottle. Make sure you drink all the drink first (probably not all in one go though!)
• Vacuum cleaner with the cleaning head removed

WHAT YOU DO:

1 Switch on the vacuum cleaner.

2 Place the tube over the neck of the bottle.

WHAT HAPPENS:

The bottle is instantly crushed as air is sucked out.

THIS IS BECAUSE:

The bottle was crushed by the air around it! When you sucked out the air you created a vacuum – in other words nothing. The air around us crushes us with a pressure of 1 kg per square cm – just imagine balancing a bag of sugar on a stick resting on your body. Now imagine being squashed by hundreds of bags of sugar and you'll get the idea.

SUGAR

ISN'T THAT SWEET!

Bet you never knew!

Otto von Guericke used a vacuum in a famous experiment. He put two copper bowls together to make a hollow ball. Then he sucked the air from the ball. Twelve horses couldn't pull the ball apart even though it was only held together by the air!

A BREATH OF FRESH AIR

DANIEL BERNOULLI KNEW **ALL** ABOUT AIRFLOW.

YOU MEAN HE WAS FULL OF HOT AIR?

JUST FOR THAT YOU CAN BLOW UP THESE BALLOONS!

WHAT YOU NEED:

• Two balloons blown up to the same size – about 18 cm across
• Two identical lengths of string (about 80 cm long)
• Blu-tack
• Doorway
• Drinking straw

BRAINY BREAKTHROUGH

NAME: DANIEL BERNOULLI (1700–1782)
NATIONALITY: SWISS

Daniel Bernoulli was a mathematician. He didn't do experiments, but later experiments showed that his findings about the link between the speed a liquid (or air) is flowing and its pressure were quite right. Why not check them for yourself?

DON'T BLOW TOO HARD, MONSTER BOY!

BANG

WHAT YOU DO:

1 Tie a length of string to the neck of each balloon.

2 Use blu tack to stick the string to the lintel of the door so that the balloons hang down about 12 cm apart and level with your head.

3 Put the end of the straw exactly midway between the balloons and blow gently.

4 Now blow harder.

WHAT HAPPENS:

The harder you blow the more the balloons move together. (If one balloon moves more than the other the straw may not be pointing midway between them.)

AIR PRESSURE FROM THE SIDES PUSHES THE BALLOONS TOGETHER

AIR FLOWS FASTER BETWEEN THE BALLOONS = LESS AIR PRESSURE

THIS IS BECAUSE:

As Daniel Bernoulli predicted, the faster the air flows, the less pressure it has. This Bernoulli effect actually explains why planes fly. As air flows over the curve of an aircraft wing, it speeds up. There's less air pressure over the wing than under it, and the pressure of the air under the wing is enough to lift the plane in the air.

IT'S PLANE-LY OBVIOUS.

AND HE TELLS ME OFF FOR MY JOKES!

Bet you never knew!
1 Daniel Bernoulli had the sort of dad you wouldn't wish on your worst enemy. Dan's dreadful dad forced him to study medicine when he preferred maths. And when he later became a famous mathematician his dad pinched his ideas and claimed he had thought of them first.
2 Today there's a Bernoulli crater on the Moon, but it's actually named after Dan's uncle and his scheming dad!

The GRUESOME GAS Quiz

Here are four gases found in air. Can you mix them in their correct proportions?

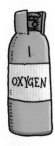   

1 — OXYGEN

2 — CARBON DIOXIDE

3 — NITROGEN

4 — ARGON

Possible proportions
a) Less than 1%.
b) 78%.
c) 21%

IMPORTANT NOTICE
1 One of these proportions can be used twice.
2 Some of these gases are poisonous in too large doses.

GET IT WRONG AND YOU'LL HAVE TO BREATHE THE MIXTURE!

Answers:
1 c), 2 a), 3 b), 4 a).

Electric Shockers

Electricity and magnetism seem shockingly mysterious, but the Baron is doing his best to explain them to Monster Boy…

BARON FRANKENSTEIN'S GUIDE TO
ELECTRICITY AND MAGNETISM

Everything is made up of atoms.
Atoms consist of a cloud of electrons
whizzing around the centre (scientists call
this centre the nucleus).

When electrons move together they produce
an electric current. Most people use
an electric current to power
TVs or CD players — I use it
to make frog's legs twitch...

Electrons also make the
electromagnetic force. This force
can pull on other atoms and we detect it
as light and magnetism.

ME GOT A-TUM.

YOU NEED A NEW BRAIN!

MONKEY BRAIN

A DIPPY DISCOVERY

WILLIAM GILBERT PROVED THE EARTH WAS A GIANT MAGNET. PERSONALLY I FIND GIANT MAGNETS IDEAL FOR CONTROLLING MONSTER BOY!

NOT SO FAST, MY BOY!

PULL

BRAINY BREAKTHROUGH

NAME: WILLIAM GILBERT (1544-1603)
NATIONALITY: BRITISH

Before William Gilbert no one understood magnetism, and some people even thought that rubbing a magnet with garlic would make the force change direction. Genius Gilbert spent 17 years doing magnetic experiments, including one with a round magnet and a smaller magnet that showed that the Earth was a giant magnet. In the next experiment you can follow in Gilbert's footsteps - but it won't take you 17 years.

WHAT YOU NEED:
- **Round flat plastic lid about 7 cm across**
- **Bar magnet**
- **Blu-tack**
- **Compass (If you don't have a compass, don't despair – you can still try this experiment. Simply stroke a needle with the same end of your magnet for about 30 seconds – this turns the needle into a magnet. Then tie your needle to a 15-cm length of thread to make a compass needle.)**
- **A large mirror on the wall**

WHAT YOU DO:

1 Stick the lid to the mirror with blu tack. Don't stick it on the wall or it may make a mess.

AND USE BLU TACK NOT BOGEYS!

2 Stick the bar magnet to the lid as shown. Congratulations – you've just made a model of the Earth! The magnetic force comes from one end or "pole" of the magnet and arches around towards the other.

3 Move your compass around the magnet (if you're using a homemade compass you'll be holding the thread). Try to keep the needle at the same distance from the magnet – about 2 cm.

WHAT HAPPENS:

The end of the needle dips towards each pole of the magnet.

THIS IS BECAUSE:

The magnetic compass needle is lining up with the magnetic force from the larger magnet. Magnetism is amazing isn't it?

IT SURE IS!

AGGH – MY WATCH!

Bet you never knew!

1. William Gilbert was a clever man but he could never decide how to spell his name – sometimes he spelt it "Gilberd".

2. William Gilbert was England's top doctor and looked after Queen Elizabeth I. Sadly the Queen died shortly after Gilbert became her doc. And then Gilbert himself died of a disease he couldn't cure.

gilbert   gillburd   gilbirt

gillb

A SHINING EXAMPLE

DRACULA HAS ASKED ME TO CLEAN HIS SILVER CANDLESTICKS BUT I HAVE A WICKED IDEA TO SAVE EFFORT. AND FOR ONCE IT DOESN'T INVOLVE GETTING MONSTER BOY TO DO THE HARD WORK!

PHEW!

I'M GOING TO GET HUMPHRY DAVY TO HELP.

BUT I THOUGHT HE WAS DEAD?

BRAINY BREAKTHROUGH

Name: Humphry Davy (1778–1829)
Nationality: British

Humphry Davy was the first person to find out how passing an electric current through a substance could rip molecules apart. He used it to discover what type of atoms a substance was made of. Fancy giving it a go?

WHAT YOU NEED:

- **Some disgustingly blackened silverware (check with your pet adult before helping yourself to family heirlooms)**
- **Pet adult**
- **An ovenproof baking dish**
- **Kitchen foil**
- **Kettle**
- **Baking soda**
- **Spoon**
- **Clean cloth**

WHAT YOU DO:

1 Line the bottom of the dish with baking foil.

HORRIBLE DANGER!
Younger readers should order their pet adult to undertake this dangerous task.

2 Lay the silver object on the foil (the two metals have to touch each other).

3 Boil a kettleful of water. Carefully pour the water over the silver to completely cover it.

4 Quickly mix in a tablespoonful of baking soda and stir it well.

WHAT HAPPENS:

The mixture froths and
doesn't smell too good.
Underneath the froth, the water
turns grey as the black stuff vanishes from
the silver and starts to appear on the foil. Leave
the water to cool and then remove the silver and wipe it
clean with the cloth. If some of the tarnish is left, you
may need to repeat the experiment.

THIS IS BECAUSE:

*Tarnish is made up of silver and sulpher atoms that have
combined to form silver sulphide molecules (groups of
atoms). The experiment sent an electric current zapping
from the foil to the silver to split the molecules. The
sulphur atoms are forced off the silver – leaving the
silverware clean – and on to the foil, which is why it
becomes darker.*

I LOVE THIS EXPERIMENT!

IT'S CERTAINLY BRIGHTENED HIM UP.

MIKE'S MOTOR

MONSTER BOY IS GOING TO SHOW US AN EXPERIMENT INSPIRED BY MICHAEL FARADAY'S ELECTRIC MOTOR. MEANWHILE I'LL USE THE ELECTRIC MOTOR IN THIS BLENDER TO MAKE BODY SOUP FOR HIS TEA.

DON'T FORGET THE EYEBALLS!

BRAINY BREAKTHROUGH

Name: Michael Faraday (1791-1867)
Nationality: British

Scientists already knew that an electric current creates a magnetic force. Fantastic Faraday combined a current and magnet to make a motor. Here's how he discovered that what goes around really does come around – again and again and again!

WHAT YOU NEED:

- **Balloon**
- **Four round magnets**
- **Bar magnet**
- **Sticky tape**
- **Tape measure**
- **Drawing pin**
- **String and scissors**
- **Doorway**

HURRY UP, MONSTER BOY!

WHAT YOU DO:

1 Blow up the balloon and tie the end.

2 Use sticky tape to stick the round magnets, evenly spaced, around the middle of the balloon as shown.

3 Make sure the magnets have the same pole facing outwards – you can check this by touching each round magnet with one end of your bar magnet. You need to use the end of the round magnet that pushes away the bar magnet. Use the tape measure to check the magnets are the same distance apart.

4 Tie the string to the balloon. Use the drawing pin to hang the string and balloon from the top of the open doorway.

5 Gently stroke the air 2–3 cm from the balloon magnets with the same end of your bar magnet.

WHAT HAPPENS:

The balloon starts to spin round.

THIS IS BECAUSE:

> EVERY MAGNET HAS A NORTH AND A SOUTH POLE.

The magnetic force always comes from the north pole and goes to the south. If you push two north or two south poles together, the force will pushes them apart. The magnetic forces pushed the balloon around to the next magnet and so on – making the balloon spin. In Faraday's 1831 experiment, some copper wire became magnetic when an electric current was run through it, and the two magnetic forces pushed the wire around the pole of a fixed magnet in the same way. It was a simple electric motor.

MAGNETIC FORCES MAKE BALLOON SPIN

SPOT THE DIFFERENCE

SCIENCE MAKES MONSTER'S HEAD SPIN

Bet you never knew!

Michael Faraday later found out that you could use a moving magnet to make an electric current too. So I guess he was into "current affairs", ha ha!

COULD YOU BE A FAMOUS Scientist?

So how would you measure up against the best and brightest of the science world?

1 British boffin Henry Cavendish (1731–1810) is famous for discovering hydrogen gas. How did he test electric currents?
a) By eating them.
b) By giving himself painful shocks.

2 How did William Gilbert test the old ideas that magnets are affected by garlic and can cure a headache?
a) Experiments.
b) He believed the ideas – so he didn't test them.

3 How did Humphry Davy test new gases?
a) He put his pet hamster in a goldfish bowl and made it breathe the gases.
b) He sniffed them himself.

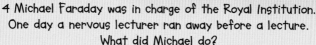

4 Michael Faraday was in charge of the Royal Institution. One day a nervous lecturer ran away before a lecture. What did Michael do?

a) Entertained the audience by telling them about his aunt's toenail operation.

b) He made up a speech as he went along and came up with a great new science idea.

5 German scientist Heinrich Hertz (1856–1894) discovered radio waves using electric sparks. A student asked Hertz what was the use of radio waves. How did he reply?

a) "Nothing, really."

b) "One day they will be used to send music and pictures all around the world."

Answers:

1 b) The more painful the stronger the current. Don't try this at home – and don't try it on small furry pets or brothers and sisters either.

2 a) If you want to check them yourself try walking around chewing garlic with a magnet tied to your head.

3 b) Don't try this at home – this horrible habit helped to bring Davy to a fairly early grave.

4 b) Faraday suggested that light is made of electric and magnetic waves. He made up the idea on the spur of the moment but he was totally right!

5 a) He never imagined TV or radio.

Baffling Biology

If physics can be foul and freaky, biology can be barmy and baffling. No wonder scientists had such a hard time seeing the wood from the trees.

CRUNCH

HAVE A
HEART!

OH HORRORS – WE'VE RUN OUT OF BLOOD! WHAT CAN WE GIVE COUNT DRACULA FOR TEA?

DON'T LOOK AT ME.

NOR ME

I KNOW – WE'LL MAKE SOME BLOOD AND I'LL TELL YOU ABOUT WILLIAM HARVEY.

PHEW!!

BRAINY BREAKTHROUGH

NAME: WILLIAM HARVEY (1578–1657)
NATIONALITY: BRITISH

Before William Harvey, most doctors thought that blood was made in the liver and heart and eaten up by the body. But wise William pointed out that the liver would have to make tonnes of blood to keep the body supplied. He said the blood went round the body – and he proved it by studying blood moving in the arteries (away from the heart) and veins (towards the heart). Here's how to see the difference in artery and vein blood for yourself...

DON'T PANIC! It's not real blood – honest!

WHAT YOU NEED:

- **Flour**
- **Dessert spoon**
- **2 sinister goblets for drinking blood from** (well, that's what the Baron uses but 2 ordinary glasses will do)
- **Red and green food colouring**
- **100 ml warm water in a measuring jug**
- **Golden syrup**
- **Tablespoon**
- **Wooden spoon**

TRY IT IF YOU THINK YOU'RE BRAVE ENOUGH!

WHAT YOU DO:

1 Mix 2 dessertspoonfuls of flour with the water and stir well until the flour has dissolved.

2 Add a heaped dessertspoonful of syrup and stir well, again until the syrup has mixed with the liquid.

3 Add one tablespoonful of red food colouring and stir well. Now you've got some homemade blood…

HORRIBLE MESS!
Food colouring stains clothes and hands just as much as blood. Wear old clothes for this experiment!

4 Pour half the blood into one of your glasses.

5 Now add a drop of green colour to the jug and pour the rest of the mixture into the second glass.

WHAT HAPPENS:

You've made a glass of revoltingly realistic bright-red "blood" and a glass of purply red "blood". Why not sample them?

DON'T MIND IF I DO...

THIS IS BECAUSE:

Blood in the arteries is bright red because it contains oxygen molecules sucked in by the lungs. Your body uses the oxygen to release energy. In the veins the blood is dark red (it even looks blue under fair skin) because it contains less oxygen. The colour difference is a clue that the lungs are involved in the circulation of blood and that the body uses oxygen in some way. But Harvey never worked out exactly how the body used blood.

After the experiment you can invite your friends for a blood feast!

YOUR VERY BAD HEALTH!

CHINK

CHEERS!

PANTING PLANTS

I'M GOING TO SHOW YOU HOW STEPHEN HALES FOUND OUT HOW PLANTS USE WATER. AND THEN YOU CAN WATER MY MAN-EATING VENUS' FLYTRAPS.

GROAN!

BRAINY BREAKTHROUGH

NAME: STEPHEN HALES (1677-1761)
NATIONALITY: BRITISH

Before Stephen Hales started experimenting on plants, people thought that water circulated inside a plant like blood in the human body. By cutting branches and placing them in water, sensible Stephen showed that movement was one way — from the roots to the leaves. Anyway — this experiment should point you in the right direction.

WHAT YOU NEED:

- **Stalk of celery – complete with leaves**
- **100 ml water in a glass**
- **Red food colouring**
- **Sharp knife**
- **Pet adult**

DON'T EAT IT, YOU NAUGHTY MONSTER!

CRUNCH

MUNCH

WHAT YOU DO:

1 Mix enough red food colouring in the water to make it a tasteful blood-red colour.

THAT'S NOT BLOOD, MONSTER BOY!

SLURP!

2 Cut the bottom off the celery stalk in a straight line so that the end of the stem is level.

HORRIBLE DANGER!

Younger readers should order their pet adult to do the difficult and dangerous cutting work.

3 Place the stem in the water for ten minutes.

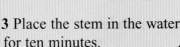

2 mm

4 Now for the tricky bit. Cut the celery like this about 3 cm from the bottom of the stem…

5 Now lean the top part of the stem over so you get a good view of the stringy bits that are keeping the two

parts of the celery stem together. Lean
the stem over some more and peel back
the skin on each part of the celery.

WHAT HAPPENS:
The stringy bits contain red. In other words…

THIS IS BECAUSE:

THE PLANT DRINKS BLOOD?

FOOLISH BOY.
I TOLD YOU –
IT'S NOT BLOOD!

*The water has been drawn up tiny tubes towards the
celery leaves. All plants do this, and scientists call it
transpiration.*

SPOT THE DIFFERENCE

SUCK
SLURP

TRANSPIRATION

PERSPIRATION

Bet you never knew!
Hales was also an inventor. He invented a surgical tool for
crushing bladder stones (sounds painful!) and a pair of
giant bellows for wafting fresh air into smelly prisons.
Could your school toilets do with this essential invention?

EVOLUTION SOLUTION

I LOVE MAKING MONSTERS USING BODY BITS. BUT NATURE MAKES NEW LIFEFORMS THROUGH EVOLUTION, AS CHARLES DARWIN FOUND OUT...

I NEED A CAT'S TAIL...

TIME I WASN'T HERE!

BRAINY BREAKTHROUGH

NAME: CHARLES DARWIN (1809-1882)
NATIONALITY: BRITISH

Why were the animals and plants around at the time of the dinosaurs different to now? Where do new plants and animals come from? After years of study Charles Darwin realized that lifeforms change over time, but you can make it happen in a few minutes...

WHAT YOU NEED:

• Jar of coloured paper clips
• A3 sheet of coloured paper (or 2 A4 pieces put together)
(I used blue but the Baron
prefers blood red for some
strange reason)
• Magnet (ideally a round one
with a hole in it)
• 30 cm string
• Notepad and pencil
• Dark, gloomy corner of
your home

I USED MY DUNGEONS...

WHAT YOU DO:

1 Tie the string to the magnet. If you like, you can tie the
other end of the string to a stick to make a fishing rod
but this isn't vital.

2 Place the paper in the dark, gloomy corner (it helps if
it's getting dark or you draw the curtains).

3 Place 20 light-coloured paperclips and 20 dark ones on
the paper. I used blue and white paperclips. Make sure
the clips are spread evenly on the paper.

4 YOU are a fierce dangerous creature that hunts at dusk.
The paperclips are your favourite prey. To hunt, you need
to lower your magnetic grab so that it touches the paper
but you can only do this FIVE times before you put on
the light.

5 Write down the number of light and dark clips you caught.

6 Count the number of light and dark clips left on the paper. Add one dark clip for every dark clip left and one light clip for every light clip left.

7 Then repeat steps 4–6 a few more times.

YOU DON'T NEED TO EAT THE CLIPS, MONSTER BOY!

WHAT HAPPENS:
After a while there are few, if any, light clips left on the paper.

THIS IS BECAUSE:
Just like a real animal, the paper clip beast survives best if it's hard to spot. That way it avoids ending up as a tasty snack for a hungry hunter. By adding a clip for each survivor you're creating what Darwin called "natural selection". The surviving animals have a chance to breed and pass on their features, and the ones that get eaten don't. This is how lifeforms change over time – a process scientists call "evolution".

Bet you never knew!

One day Darwin was collecting beetles. He caught one beetle in each hand. Then, he caught a third, more interesting, beetle and put it in his mouth. But the battling beetle made a foul chemical and when dopey Darwin spat it out, all the beetles escaped. Don't try this at home – as Darwin didn't say...

A BIT OF BREEDING

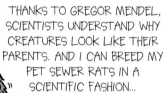

THANKS TO GREGOR MENDEL, SCIENTISTS UNDERSTAND WHY CREATURES LOOK LIKE THEIR PARENTS. AND I CAN BREED MY PET SEWER RATS IN A SCIENTIFIC FASHION...

BRAINY BREAKTHROUGH

NAME: GREGOR MENDEL (1822–1884)
NATIONALITY: BORN IN PRESENT-DAY CZECH REPUBLIC

Charles Darwin had explained evolution, but even the great man was a bit shaky on how living things passed on their features to their offspring. The man who sorted out this mystery was a pea-brained monk. Well, he must have been because in seven years he bred 28,000 pea-plants. In the end he found out that there's a vital rule that explains how features known as "genes" are passed on, and he founded a new science called "genetics". Could you make the same discovery?

DON'T PANIC, readers, you don't have to plant thousands of boring old pea plants. NO — you'll be working with the Baron's GIANT FLESH-EATING SEWER RATS — Oh-er, I'm off!

WHAT YOU NEED:

- **This book**
- **Photocopier**
- **Scissors**
- **Black pen**

WHAT YOU DO:

1 Photocopy this page four times and cut out the cards. (If you're feeling creative you could draw your own cards.)

2 At the moment you've got four white rats and four black rats, but for this experiment you'll need two white rats and six black rats. Using your black pen, turn two white rats into black rats. Then fill in both the circles beneath your new black rats.

3 Cut out all your rat cards.

4 Now read these rules…

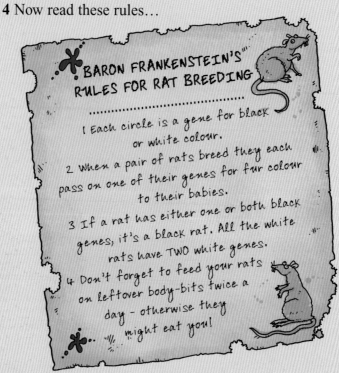

BARON FRANKENSTEIN'S RULES FOR RAT BREEDING

1 Each circle is a gene for black or white colour.

2 When a pair of rats breed they each pass on one of their genes for fur colour to their babies.

3 If a rat has either one or both black genes, it's a black rat. All the white rats have TWO white genes.

4 Don't forget to feed your rats on leftover body-bits twice a day – otherwise they might eat you!

5 Start with a white rat and a black rat with two black circles. Lay the cards face up on a table.

6 The rats have two babies. You will need to work out what colour the babies are going to be.

7 The pair of young rats have four babies. Notice what genes the babies have. What colour are the rats?

WHAT HAPPENS:

The first pair of rats produced two black rat babies. The babies produced three baby black rats and one white rat.

THIS IS BECAUSE:

This is exactly what Mendel found. He had proved that certain features (now known as genes) cancel out others, but that the effect of the cancelled-out gene pops up in the second generation in a ratio of 1 to 3. Not bad for a pea-brain, huh?

WHAT WOULD I GET IF I CROSSED MY EYEBALLS?

NO – I WOULD GET EYESTRAIN.

EYE COLOUR IS INHERITED IN A SIMILAR WAY...

GRR – FOOLISH BOY!

Bet you never knew!

At first no one took any notice of Mendel's dramatic discovery. Scientists only began to sit up and take notice 40 years later – but Mendel was dead by then. I expect he was pushing up the pea-plants.

The MAD MISSING LINK Quiz

In a bid to find out how the heart worked, William Harvey cut open a live pigeon. When the heart stopped he put 1_____ on his 2 _____ and touched it. The heart started.

Stephen Hales was also interested in the body. He let all the 3____ out of a sheep and filled its heart with 4_____ to measure how much it could pump.

Charles Darwin encouraged his children to put 5_____ on bumblebees and follow them to find out where they went.

Missing words
a) Wax
b) Spit
c) Blood
d) Finger
e) Flour

DON'T BE SHEEPISH!

Answers:
1b), 2d) The warmth started the heart beating.
3c), 4a), 5e)

The Crucial Cosmos

Some scientists aren't happy with little discoveries. They want to understand the BIG PICTURE that explains the entire unbelievable universe. Let's meet these big-headed boffins…

HOW HORRIBLY FASCINATING!

ON THE CARDS

HERE'S A CARD GAME BASED ON HOW DMITRI MENDELEYEV SORTED THE ELEMENTS*...

IT SOUNDS HARD.

DON'T WORRY – ELEMENT–ARY!

WHAT YOU NEED:
- **This book**
- **Scissors**
- **Photocopier**
- **A good friend**

(but in an emergency your long-suffering pet adult will do)

- **Notebook and pencil**

*An element is a type of atom such as gold or oxygen.

BRAINY BREAKTHROUGH

NAME: DMITRI MENDELEYEV (1834-1907)
NATIONALITY: RUSSIAN

Dmitri Mendeleyev was a big fan of the card game Patience, and that's where he got the idea of writing the names of elements on cards and putting them in weight order. Dmitri created a crucial chart called the Periodic Table,  and the number patterns in this tremendous table are a code that explains why certain chemicals combine to create chemical changes. Here's your chance to crack the code...

WHAT YOU DO:

1 Photocopy the next page – ideally on to thin card.

2 Cut out the squares. Each one is a card for the game.

3 Read the rules and play the game.

GRR – CUT OUT THE PHOTOCOPY NOT THE BOOK, MONSTER BOY!

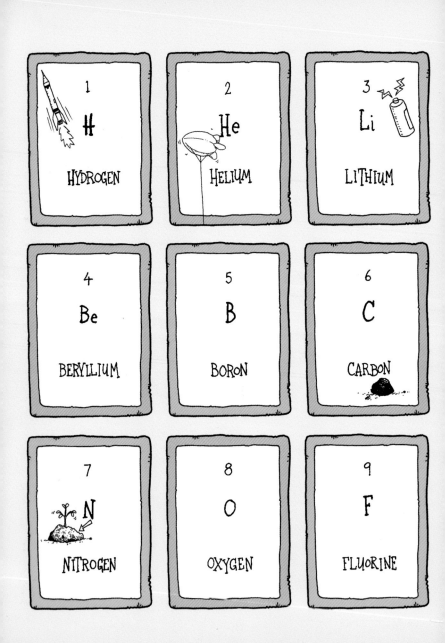

10	11	12
Ne 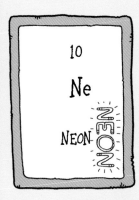 NEON	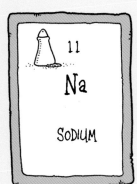 Na SODIUM	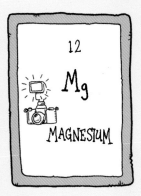 Mg MAGNESIUM

13	14	15
 Al ALUMINIUM	Si  SILICON	P PHOSPHORUS

16	17	18
 S SULPHUR	Cl  CHLORINE	 Ar ARGON

ATOMIC EIGHTS

RULES OF THE GAME

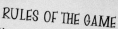

1 Shuffle the cards. Give yourself and your friend 9 cards each.

2 The player with the H = hydrogen starts off by laying this card face up. They are followed by the player with the He = Helium card. The player with the Li = Lithium card places it under the Hydrogen card (of course the same player might have all of these cards!)

3 The players each then play a card in turn — the aim is to form as many columns of 2 or 3 as you can.

HINT — You can tell which cards go in which column because the lower card is 8 more than the upper. So if you had Be = Beryllium which is 4 you would need Mg = Magnesium to make a column.

4 A player scores TWO points for completing a column of two and THREE points for completing a column of three. But if they put a card in the wrong place they LOSE one point! Write down your scores in the notebook.

5 The game ends when one of the players runs out of cards.

I WON!

YOU CHEATED!

SPOT THE BAD LOSER

4 After the game lay down all the cards to complete the columns. Arrange the columns so that the rows are in order of number – so Li will be next to Be and Na next to Mg and so on.

WHAT HAPPENS:

You've actually made a copy of part of the Periodic Table!

IS IT HORRIBLY COMPLICATED?

YOU'LL BE SORRY YOU ASKED...

THIS IS BECAUSE:

The number of an element (scientists call this the atomic number) is in order of weight – hydrogen is the lightest, so it's number 1. The elements in each column combine with other elements in a similar way.

"But why?" I hear you wondering.
"And is it to do with the number 8?"
Well, yes it is. Imagine two atoms combining to form a molecule...
Well, to do it, the elements in your game need to share a total of – wait for it – EIGHT electrons! Mind you, Mendeleyev didn't know about all this – electrons hadn't been discovered in his day!

LET'S GET TOGETHER.

OK!

DUH...

Bet you never knew!

Dmitri Mendeleyev was an amazing man. He only had his hair cut once a year and then it was with sheep shears. When he lost his temper he used to dance about with rage. Don't get any ideas — dancing around with a scary haircut won't convince anyone that you're a genius.

A 'HOLE' LOT OF THINKING

ALBERT EINSTEIN'S WORK SHOWED THAT A BLACK HOLE IS LIKE A PLUGHOLE...

YOU MEAN CLOGGED UP WITH BITS OF HAIR AND FINGERNAILS?

FOOLISH BOY! PAY ATTENTION – YOU MIGHT LEARN SOMETHING!

BRAINY BREAKTHROUGH

NAME: ALBERT EINSTEIN (1879-1955)
NATIONALITY: GERMAN-BORN, AMERICAN

Albert Einstein didn't need a lab to do experiments – he did them in his head! These exercises are called thought experiments and you do them by imagining what would happen if you could, for example, surf on a beam of light. Amazing Albert then put his ideas in a mathematical form. He found out that gravity takes the form of the bending of space around an object. This was the basis of his greatest idea – the Theory of Relativity. Einstein's ideas have been proven again and again in experiments, and here's how to see them in action...

STAGE ONE

WHAT YOU NEED:

Round bowl (as large as possible – up to 30 cm across)
- **Peppercorns**
- **Round heavy object**
(I used a tomato about 2.5 cm across)
- **Clingfilm**

AND I USED THIS SKULL!

WHAT YOU DO:

1 Stretch the clingfilm across the top of the bowl as tightly as you can.

FLICK

WHIZZZ

2 Place the round object in the middle of the clingfilm. It will make a slight dip.

3 Now for the skilful bit. Your tomato (or whatever it is) is an alien planet. The peppercorn is your spacecraft. Can you roll it or gently flick it with your finger so that it passes close by Planet Tomato without crashing into it?

WHAT HAPPENS:

The spacecraft appears drawn to the planet – but with skill and enough speed you can get past it.

THIS IS BECAUSE:

In Einstein's Theory of Relativity you can imagine gravity as a kind of dip in space caused by the planet. Rocket scientists need to consider this effect when planning space trips. If their speed or direction is wrong they could be drawn in by the planet's gravity and crash.

STAGE TWO

HMMM...

WHAT YOU NEED:
• Sink (a bathroom sink is ideal)
• 4 or 5 paper circles from a paper hole-punch

WHAT YOU DO:
1 Fill the sink with water and float the paper circles on top.

2 Now pull out the plug. The paper circles are planets and the plughole is a giant black hole. Watch what happens.

WHAT HAPPENS:
The planets whirl around the black hole going faster and faster until they're sucked in and never seen again.

THIS IS BECAUSE:

A black hole has limitless gravity, and matter really does get whirled around it and sucked in like a giant plughole. Once in the hole the planet is ripped to bits. This could happen to an astronaut too...

BRAINLESS ZOMBIES

ANY VOLUNTEERS STUPID ENOUGH TO VISIT A BLACK HOLE?

ME! ME!

Bet you never knew!

Although his work clearly predicted black holes, Einstein didn't believe they existed. Although no one has ever visited a black hole, scientists have now spotted them by the radio waves given off as gas is sucked into them...

THE BIG BLOW-UP

SPACE IS GETTING BIGGER EVERY SECOND, AS EDWIN HUBBLE FOUND OUT. IT'S A BIT LIKE THIS BUBBLE...

IT'S MADE OF SOAP?

GRR – FOOLISH BOY!

BRAINY BREAKTHROUGH

Name: Edwin Hubble (1889–1953)
Nationality: American

Before Edwin Hubble's brainy breakthrough, everyone – even top scientists such as Albert Einstein – thought that the universe had always been the same size. But by studying the light from distant galaxies, Hubble proved that they are all moving away from us – and we are moving away from them. Space is getting bigger all the time. Find out what's going on by blowing up your own universe...

WHAT YOU NEED:

- **A balloon**
- **Stick-on paper shapes (stars would be ideal)**
- **Crocodile clip or pet adult equipped with a thumb and four fingers**
- **Ruler**

I PREFER TO USE A HUMAN LUNG!

WHAT YOU DO:

1 Blow up the balloon until it's about 10 cm across.

2 Hold the neck of the balloon with the clip or order your pet adult to do this task.

3 Stick the stars or paper shapes on the balloon about 2 cm apart.

PAFF

4 Blow up the balloon some more.

WHAT HAPPENS:

The shapes are soon twice as far apart – you can check the distance with your ruler.

THIS IS BECAUSE:

The balloon gets bigger. Imagine that each shape is a galaxy and the whole thing is happening in three dimensions (yikes – this is hard!) and you'll get an idea of what's happening in the real universe.

So are you out of it too? Why not tune in with this crazy cosmic quiz?

The CRAZY COSMIC SCIENTIST Quiz

TRUE OR FALSE?

1. Dmitri Mendeleyev had the idea for the Periodic Table in a dream.

2. Albert Einstein's last words were "I've been relatively successful".

3. When Edwin Hubble left school his teacher said:

I HAVE WATCHED YOU FOR FOUR YEARS AND I HAVE NEVER SEEN YOU STUDY FOR TEN MINUTES.

Answers:

1. True – or so Mendeleyev claimed!

2. False – no one knows what they were. Einstein spoke in German and his nurse couldn't speak the language.

3. True – Hubble was brainy but he was even better at sports.

EPILOGUE:
THE STICKY END

Science is full of mistakes. There are puny little mistakes like the ones you make in your science homework...

CALL THIS A **LITTLE** MISTAKE, WATKINS?

SHAKE

DUH...

And whopping BIG BLUNDERS like the idiotic ideas that people used to have about anything from how things fell to how the blood moves in your body. Thank goodness for experiments and the great scientists who set them up and put everyone else right!

The wonderful thing about an experiment is that you can't argue with the results (and if anyone tries to argue you can always repeat the experiment and check your results). And from the results comes all the science in this book.

Hmm – there's a thought! Without the great scientists and their discoveries there would be nothing to put in this book. And that means no famously foul experiments for you to try! Oh well, I guess we've all got a lot to thank them for!